# JOHN GRISHAM

# FROM COURTROOM TO BESTSELLER

*The Definitve Biography*

Orion Vale

**Copyright © 2024 Orion Vale**

All right reserved. No part of this book may be reproduced, distributed, or transmitted in any form or by any means, including photocopying, recording, or other electronic or mechanical methods, without the prior written permission of the publisher, except in the case of brief quotations embodied in critical reviews and certain other non-commercial uses permitted by copyright law.

# TABLE OF CONTENT

FOREWORD ..................................................................... 4

INTRODUCTION ............................................................ 16

CHAPTER ONE ............................................................... 29

    Southern Roots: The Early Years ............................... 29

CHAPTER TWO ............................................................... 34

    The Young Lawyer: Building a Career ...................... 34

CHAPTER THREE .......................................................... 41

    A Time to kill: The Birth of a Writer ......................... 41

CHAPTER FOUR ............................................................ 49

    The Firm and Beyond: Rise to Literary Stardom ........ 49

CHAPTER FIVE .............................................................. 56

    Broadening Horizons: Exploring New Territories ....... 56

CHAPTER SIX ................................................................. 65

    The Established Author: Legacy and Continued Success
.......................................................................................... 65

CHAPTER SEVEN .......................................................... 73

    The Grisham Effect ..................................................... 73

# FOREWORD

In the pantheon of modern American literature, few names shine as brightly as John Grisham. For over three decades, Grisham has captivated millions of readers worldwide with his gripping legal thrillers, becoming a household name and a cultural touchstone.

His journey from a small-town lawyer to a literary juggernaut is not just a tale of personal triumph, but a testament to the enduring power of storytelling and the American dream. As we embark on this comprehensive exploration of John Grisham's life and career, it's worth pondering the question: What is it about Grisham's work that has resonated so deeply with readers across generations and cultures? The answer, I believe, lies in his unique ability to blend the intricate workings of the legal system with universal themes of justice, morality, and human nature.

Grisham's stories, at their core, are modern-day morality tales. They pit David against Goliath, the individual against the system, good against evil. Yet, they do so with a nuance and complexity that reflects the real world, where ethical dilemmas are rarely black and white. This moral ambiguity, coupled with Grisham's knack for creating page-turning suspense, has proven to be an irresistible combination for readers.

But Grisham's impact extends far beyond the realm of entertainment. His works have shed light on important social and legal issues, from the death penalty to corporate malfeasance, insurance fraud to racial injustice. In doing so, he has not only educated millions of readers about the intricacies of the legal system but has also sparked important conversations about justice and ethics in society at large.

The story of John Grisham Is, in many ways, quintessentially American. Born in Jonesboro, Arkansas, in 1955, Grisham's early years were marked by frequent moves as his family followed his father's construction work. This nomadic childhood, spanning several Southern states, would later inform the rich, atmospheric settings of his novels.

Despite his peripatetic upbringing, Grisham's family instilled in him a love for reading and a strong work ethic.

His mother, a homemaker, was a voracious reader who encouraged her children to explore the world through books. His father, while not a reader himself, emphasized the importance of education and hard work. These early influences would prove crucial in shaping Grisham's future path.

Grisham's journey to becoming a writer was far from direct. After briefly considering a career in professional baseball—a passion that would later manifest in his novel *A Painted House* he pursued a degree in accounting at Mississippi State University. It was during this time that Grisham first entertained the idea of becoming a tax lawyer, a career path that seemed to promise financial stability.

However, as he progressed through his studies, Grisham found himself increasingly drawn to criminal law. The drama of the courtroom, the high stakes involved, and the opportunity to make a tangible difference in people's lives all appealed to his sense of justice and his growing interest in the complexities of human nature. This shift in focus would prove pivotal, not just for his legal career, but for his future as a writer.

After graduating from law school at the University of Mississippi in 1981, Grisham began practicing law in Southaven, Mississippi. For nearly a decade, he balanced a busy legal career with his responsibilities as a state legislator, representing his district in the Mississippi House of Representatives from 1984 to 1990. It was during this period that the seed of his writing career was planted.

The Inspiration for Grisham's first novel, *A Time to kill*, came from a harrowing court case he witnessed in 1984. The case involved the rape of a young girl, and Grisham found himself imagining what would happen if the girl's father took justice into his own hands. This spark of an idea refused to let go, and Grisham began rising at 5 a.m. each day to write before heading to the office.

The process of writing *A Time to kill* was a gruelling three-year journey, snatching moments to write between court appearances, legislative sessions, and family obligations. The manuscript was rejected by numerous publishers before finally being accepted by the small Wynwood Press, which published the book in 1988 with a modest initial print run of 5,000 copies. While *A Time to kill* didn't immediately catapult Grisham to literary stardom, it did something arguably more important: it proved to him that he could write a novel. Undeterred by the modest sales of his debut, Grisham immediately began work on his second book, *The Firm*.

It was *The Firm* that would change everything. Published in 1991, the novel became a runaway bestseller, spending 47 weeks on The New York Times bestseller list and selling more than seven million copies. The book's success was amplified by its adaptation into a hit film starring Tom Cruise in 1993, cementing Grisham's place in the public consciousness.

The success of *The Firm* marked a turning point in Grisham's life. In 1991, he gave up his law practice to become a full-time writer, a decision that would lead to one of the most prolific and successful careers in modern publishing history.

Over the next three decades, Grisham would publish a new novel almost every year, with many of them becoming instant bestsellers. His legal thrillers, characterized by their fast-paced narratives, complex legal maneuverings, and exploration of moral dilemmas, became a genre unto themselves. Titles like *The Pelican Brief*, *The Client*, *The Rainmaker*, and *The Street Lawyer* not only dominated bestseller lists but also became successful Hollywood adaptations, further expanding Grisham's reach and influence.

What sets Grisham apart from many of his contemporaries is not just his consistent output, but the quality and depth of his work. While his novels are undeniably entertaining, they also grapple with serious issues. Through his fiction, Grisham has tackled topics such as the death penalty *The Chamber*, insurance fraud *The Rainmaker*, homelessness *The Street Lawyer*, and environmental destruction *The Pelican Brief*.

This combination of entertainment and social commentary has made Grisham's works more than just popular fiction they have become a lens through which millions of readers have come to understand complex legal and social issues. In many ways, Grisham has done more to educate the general public about the American legal system than any civics class or legal textbook. But Grisham's impact extends beyond his legal thrillers. As his career progressed, he began to explore other genres and styles of writing. *A Painted House* (2001), a semi-autobiographical novel set in rural Arkansas in the 1950s, showcased Grisham's ability to craft compelling narratives outside the courtroom. *Skipping Christmas* (2001), a humorous novella, demonstrated his versatility as a writer. His Theodore Boone series, aimed at young adults, has introduced a new generation of readers to the intricacies of the legal system.

Throughout his career, Grisham has remained true to his roots. He continues to live in the South, splitting his time between homes in Oxford, Mississippi, and Charlottesville, Virginia. His Southern upbringing informs much of his work, from the settings of his novels to the values and dilemmas faced by his characters.

Grisham's success has allowed him to give back in significant ways. He has been a long-time supporter of the Innocence Project, which works to exonerate wrongfully convicted individuals through DNA testing. His interest in this cause is reflected in his 2006 non-fiction book *The Innocent Man*, which tells the story of Ron Williamson, a man wrongfully convicted of murder who spent 11 years on death row before being exonerated.

In addition to his philanthropic efforts, Grisham has used his platform to advocate for various causes, including literacy, education, and criminal justice reform. He has donated millions to various charities and established scholarships at several universities.

As we delve into this biography, it's important to recognize that John Grisham's story is more than just a tale of literary success. It's a story about the power of perseverance, the impact of storytelling, and the ability of one person to make a difference in the world.

From his early days as a struggling lawyer trying to balance his legal career with his writing ambitions, to his current status as one of the world's bestselling authors, Grisham's journey offers valuable lessons about pursuing one's passions and using one's talents for the greater good.

This biography aims to provide a comprehensive look at John Grisham's life and career, exploring the experiences that shaped him, the creative process behind his works, and the impact he has had on literature and society. Through interviews with Grisham himself, his family, friends, and colleagues, as well as extensive research into his life and works, we aim to paint a full picture of the man behind the bestsellers. We'll explore Grisham's childhood in the South, his early career as a lawyer and state legislator, his struggles to get his first novel published, and his meteoric rise to literary stardom. We'll delve into his writing process, examining how he crafts his intricate plots and memorable characters. We'll also look at the real-life cases and issues that have inspired many of his novels, and how his work has, in turn, influenced public perception of the legal system.

Beyond his writing, we'll explore Grisham's personal life, his philanthropy, and his ongoing commitment to social justice. We'll examine his legacy, both as a writer and as a public figure, and consider his place in the canon of American literature.

This biography is not just for fans of John Grisham's novels. It's for anyone interested in the craft of writing, the workings of the publishing industry, or the power of literature to shape public discourse. It's for aspiring writers looking for inspiration and guidance. It's for readers curious about the man behind some of the most popular books of the past three decades.

As we embark on this journey through John Grisham's life and career, we invite you to consider the broader implications of his work. How has Grisham's writing changed the landscape of popular fiction? How has it influenced public perception of the legal system? What can his career teach us about the relationship between art and social responsibility?

In many ways, John Grisham's story is a microcosm of late 20th and early 21st century America. Through his life and work, we can trace the evolution of the publishing industry in the digital age, the changing role of the author in society, and the ongoing conversation about justice and morality in America.

As you read this biography, we encourage you to think critically about Grisham's work and its place in contemporary culture. Consider the themes that recur throughout his novels justice, corruption, redemption, the power of the individual to effect change. How do these themes resonate with your own experiences and understanding of the world?

We also invite you to reflect on the nature of storytelling itself. What is it about Grisham's narratives that have captivated millions of readers worldwide? How does he balance entertainment with social commentary? What can his approach to storytelling teach us about effective communication and persuasion?

In the chapters that follow, we'll trace John Grisham's journey from a small-town lawyer to a literary phenomenon. We'll explore the triumphs and challenges he's faced along the way, the evolution of his craft, and the impact he's had on the world beyond the page.

Whether you're a long-time fan of Grisham's work or new to his writing, we hope this biography will offer fresh insights into the life and mind of one of America's most successful and influential authors. More than that, we hope it will inspire you to consider your own potential to make a difference in the world, whether through writing, advocacy, or any other passion you may pursue.

John Grisham's story is, in many ways, still being written. As he continues to produce novels that top bestseller lists and tackle important social issues, his influence on literature and society continues to evolve. This biography aims to capture the essence of the man and his work up to this point, while also considering the potential future impact of his ongoing career.

As we delve into the life and work of John Grisham, let us remember that behind every bestseller is a person complex, flawed, and deeply human. It is this humanity, perhaps more than anything else that makes Grisham's stories so compelling and his career so inspiring.

# INTRODUCTION

In the quiet predawn hours of a crisp Mississippi morning in 1984, a young lawyer named John Grisham sat at his desk, pen in hand, embarking on a journey that would change the landscape of American literature. The courtrooms were still hours from stirring, the legal briefs could wait, and in these stolen moments, a storyteller was born.

This scene, replayed countless times over three years, would result in *A Time to kill*, Grisham's debut novel. While its initial reception was modest, it marked the beginning of a literary career that would captivate millions and redefine the legal thriller genre. But to truly understand the phenomenon that is John Grisham, we must look beyond the bestseller lists and Hollywood adaptations. We must explore the intersection of law and literature, of Southern roots and global appeal, of personal conviction and universal themes.

John Ray Grisham Jr. was born on February 8, 1955, in Jonesboro, Arkansas. The second of five siblings, young John's childhood was marked by frequent moves as his father, a construction worker and cotton farmer, sought work across the Southern United States. This nomadic existence, while challenging, imbued Grisham with a deep understanding of Southern culture and a keen eye for the nuances of small-town life – elements that would later become hallmarks of his fiction.

Despite the family's modest means, Grisham's parents placed a high value on education. His mother, Wanda, was a homemaker with a passion for reading, a love she passed on to her children. It was she who first introduced John to the works of John Steinbeck and other literary giants, planting the seeds of a lifelong love affair with storytelling.

As a child, Grisham dreamed not of courtroom dramas or bestselling novels, but of baseball diamonds. His passion for the sport was all-consuming, and for years, he harbored hopes of a professional career. This early love would later find expression in works like *A Painted House* and "Calico Joe," reminding us that while Grisham may be best known for his legal thrillers, his range as a storyteller extends far beyond the confines of the courtroom. It was during his undergraduate years at Mississippi State University that

Grisham's path began to take shape. Initially pursuing a degree in accounting with vague notions of becoming a tax lawyer, Grisham found himself increasingly drawn to the drama and high stakes of criminal law. This shift in focus would prove pivotal, not just for his legal career, but for the stories he would later tell.

After earning his Juris Doctor from the University of Mississippi School of Law in 1981, Grisham set up a small private practice in Southaven, Mississippi. For nearly a decade, he balanced his legal career with service as a Democratic member of the Mississippi House of Representatives. This dual role as lawyer and legislator provided Grisham with a unique vantage point from which to observe the intersections of law, politics, and human nature – a perspective that would deeply inform his future novels.

It was during this period that the spark of Grisham's writing career was ignited. In 1984, he witnessed a heart-wrenching testimony of a twelve-year-old rape victim in the DeSoto County courthouse. The raw emotion and injustice of the scene haunted Grisham, prompting him to wonder: What if the girl's father had taken justice into his own hands? This question became the seed from which *A Time to kill* would grow.

For the next three years, Grisham devoted his early morning hours to writing, often rising at 5 a.m. to squeeze in time at the typewriter before heading to court. This dedication in the face of a demanding career and growing family responsibilities speaks volumes about Grisham's commitment to his craft. It's a testament to the power of the story he felt compelled to tell, and to the discipline that would later enable him to produce a novel nearly every year for three decades.

The path to publication for *A Time to kill* was far from smooth. Rejected by dozens of publishers and agents, the manuscript seemed destined for obscurity until it was finally picked up by the small Wynwood Press. Published in June 1988 with an initial print run of just 5,000 copies, the novel's early sales were modest. But for Grisham, the mere fact of holding his published work in his hands was triumph enough.

Little did he know that his next novel would change everything. *The Firm*, published in 1991, became an instant sensation, spending 47 weeks on The New York Times bestseller list and selling more than seven million copies. The subsequent film adaptation starring Tom Cruise in 1993 cemented Grisham's place in the public consciousness and launched a string of Hollywood adaptations that would bring his stories to an even wider audience.

The success of *The Firm* allowed Grisham to retire from law practice and devote himself fully to writing. What followed was one of the most prolific and consistently successful careers in modern publishing history. With titles like *The Pelican Brief*, *The Client*, *The Rainmaker*, and *The Street Lawyer*, Grisham not only dominated bestseller lists but also helped define the legal thriller genre for a generation of readers.

But to view Grisham solely through the lens of his commercial success would be to miss the deeper significance of his work. Throughout his career, Grisham has used his platform to shed light on important social and legal issues. From the death penalty in *The Chamber* to insurance fraud in *The Rainmaker*, from homelessness in *The Street Lawyer*" to wrongful convictions in "The Guardian," Grisham's novels have served as vehicles for exploring complex moral and ethical dilemmas.

This commitment to social justice extends beyond the page. Grisham has been a long-time supporter of the Innocence Project, which works to exonerate wrongfully convicted individuals through DNA testing. His interest in this cause led to his first non-fiction work, *The Innocent Man* (2006), which tells the true story of Ron Williamson, a man wrongfully convicted of murder who spent 11 years on death row before being exonerated.

Grisham's influence on popular culture and the legal profession cannot be overstated. His novels have inspired countless readers to pursue careers in law, shaped public perception of the legal system, and sparked important conversations about justice and ethics. Law professors have incorporated his books into their curricula, recognizing their value in illustrating complex legal concepts in an accessible way.

Yet, for all his success, Grisham remains rooted in the South that shaped him. He continues to live in Oxford, Mississippi, eschewing the trappings of celebrity for a quieter life focused on family, writing, and philanthropy. This connection to his roots is evident in his writing, which often features richly drawn Southern settings and characters that reflect the complexity and contradictions of the region.

As we delve deeper into Grisham's life and work in the chapters that follow, we'll explore the many facets of this remarkable storyteller. We'll examine the experiences that shaped him, the creative process behind his novels, and the impact he has had on literature and society. Through interviews with Grisham, his family, friends, and colleagues, as well as extensive research into his life and works, we aim to paint a comprehensive portrait of the man behind the bestsellers.

We'll trace Grisham's evolution as a writer, from his early struggles to find his voice to his current status as a master of his craft. We'll explore how he researches his novels, crafts his intricate plots, and creates the memorable characters that populate his stories. We'll also look at how his approach to writing has changed over the years, and how he has adapted to the evolving landscape of publishing in the digital age.

Beyond his writing, we'll examine Grisham's role as a public figure and his efforts to use his platform for good. We'll explore his philanthropic work, his advocacy for various causes, and his efforts to promote literacy and education. We'll also consider how he has navigated the challenges of fame and maintained his privacy in an increasingly public world.

Throughout this biography, we'll place Grisham's work in the broader context of American literature and popular culture. We'll consider how his novels both reflect and shape societal attitudes towards the legal system, and how they engage with larger themes of justice, morality, and human nature. We'll also examine Grisham's place in the tradition of Southern literature, exploring how his work both draws from and contributes to this rich literary heritage.

One of the most fascinating aspects of Grisham's career is his ability to balance commercial success with artistic integrity and social responsibility. Unlike many authors who find themselves pigeonholed by early success, Grisham has continually pushed himself to explore new territory.

From his forays into other genres with books like *A Painted House* and *Skipping Christmas*, to his young adult Theodore Boone series, to his short story collections, Grisham has demonstrated a willingness to take risks and challenge himself creatively.

This versatility is a testament to Grisham's fundamental gifts as a storyteller. Whether he's crafting a taut legal thriller or a nostalgic coming-of-age tale, Grisham has an uncanny ability to create characters and situations that resonate with readers. His prose, often described as lean and efficient, serves the story above all else, propelling the reader forward with a momentum that has become his trademark.

As we explore Grisham's body of work, we'll also consider the criticism he has faced. Some literary critics have dismissed his work as formulaic or lacking in literary merit. Others have questioned the accuracy of his portrayal of the legal system or criticized what they see as simplistic moral frameworks in his stories. We'll examine these critiques and Grisham's responses to them, considering how they have shaped his approach to writing over the years.

One of the most intriguing aspects of Grisham's career is the interplay between his fiction and reality. Many of his novels have been inspired by real-life cases or issues, and in turn, his fiction has sometimes influenced real-world events. We'll explore this dynamic, looking at instances where Grisham's work has impacted legal proceedings or public policy debates.

We'll also delve into Grisham's writing process, examining how he balances research and imagination in crafting his stories. From his meticulous study of legal precedents to his keen observations of human behaviour, we'll explore the various elements that come together to create a Grisham novel. We'll look at how he structures his writing day, how he approaches revisions, and how he collaborates with editors and other professionals in bringing his books to market.

Throughout this biography, we'll return to the central question of what makes Grisham's work so enduringly popular. Is it the pacing of his plots? The relatability of his characters? The moral weight of his themes? Or is it something less tangible – a particular quality of storytelling that speaks to something fundamental in the human experience?

As we consider these questions, we'll also look to the future. At the time of this writing, Grisham shows no signs of slowing down. He continues to produce novels at a prodigious rate, each one eagerly anticipated by his legion of fans. What new directions might his work take? How will he continue to evolve as a writer? And what will be the lasting impact of his contribution to American literature?

In exploring these questions and many others, this biography aims to offer a comprehensive and nuanced portrait of John Grisham the man, the writer, and the cultural phenomenon. Whether you're a long-time fan of Grisham's work or new to his writing, we hope this book will offer fresh insights and a deeper appreciation for one of America's most successful and influential authors.

As we embark on this journey through Grisham's life and career, we invite you to consider your own relationship with his work. What drew you to his books? How have they influenced your understanding of the law, of justice, of human nature? What do you hope to learn about the man behind the stories you've read?

In the chapters that follow, we'll peel back the layers of Grisham's public persona to reveal the complex individual beneath. We'll explore the contradictions and consistencies in his life and work, the triumphs and the struggles, the public figure and the private man. Through it all, we hope to illuminate not just the career of a bestselling author, but the power of storytelling to shape our understanding of the world and our place in it.

John Grisham's journey from a small-town lawyer to a literary phenomenon is more than just a success story. It's a testament to the enduring power of narrative, to the ability of one person to make a difference through words, and to the complex interplay between art, commerce, and social responsibility in modern America.

As we delve into the life and work of John Grisham, we invite you to join us in considering these larger themes. How does Grisham's career reflect and refract the cultural moments he's lived through? What can his success tell us about what we value as a society? And what lessons can we draw from his life and work about the pursuit of our own passions and the potential for storytelling to change the world?

These are the questions that will guide us as we explore the remarkable life and enduring legacy of John Grisham. So let us turn the page and begin our journey into the world of a master storyteller a world where justice and injustice collide, where ordinary individuals face extraordinary challenges, and where the power of a well-told tale can change hearts, minds, and perhaps even the course of history.

# CHAPTER ONE

## Southern Roots: The Early Years

John Ray Grisham Jr. was born on February 8, 1955, in Jonesboro, Arkansas. He spent his formative years in a modest home, the second of five children born to John Grisham Sr., a construction worker and cotton farmer, and Wanda Skidmore Grisham, a homemaker with an undeniable influence on her son's education. Life in the South during the 1950s and 60s was colored by a rural, hardworking ethos, and Grisham's early environment deeply reflected this.

Though Jonesboro was a growing town, the Grishams soon moved to Southaven, Mississippi, where John's father took on jobs as a construction worker and farmer. Southaven was small and rural, a place where summer heat blazed across endless cotton fields. The simplicity of rural life, coupled with the complex realities of Southern culture at the time, became a backdrop for John's upbringing. Mississippi was steeped in racial tensions, deeply religious communities, and a strong sense of self-reliance – values that would later shape both his worldview and writing.

John's childhood, though simple, was rich in experiences. His father, a hardworking man of few words, taught him the value of labor, while his mother, a devout Christian, imbued in him a love for reading. Wanda was a constant presence, filling their small home with books and encouraging John to read anything he could get his hands on. She introduced him to storytelling, often sharing stories from the Bible and American classics, planting the seeds of imagination that would later grow into his career as a novelist.

The Grishams were a close-knit, working-class family, and despite financial constraints, John was determined to make something of himself. His mother's insistence on education and church was foundational. Sundays were spent in church, where John absorbed the oratory skills of preachers, unknowingly sharpening his sense for dialogue and narrative structure.

John's interest in storytelling wasn't immediate. He spent his early years more focused on sports, particularly baseball, dreaming of one day playing professionally. It was a dream that many boys in the South held, where baseball was almost a religion. However, as he progressed through school, it became evident that while his athletic talents were respectable, his academic strengths were equally important.

At Southaven High School, John was a good student, if somewhat undistinguished academically. His focus was still on baseball, but his exposure to history and civics classes began sparking an interest in the legal system. His teachers recognized his intelligence, though John hadn't yet discovered the path that would define his career. But his knack for observation, understanding of human nature, and ability to weave narratives were quietly taking root.

In 1973, John Grisham enrolled at Northwest Mississippi Junior College, more out of necessity than ambition. He still held onto his baseball dream, but a few semesters in, reality struck. His skills on the field weren't going to take him to the major leagues, and it was during this time that he began considering other career paths. After transferring to Delta State University and later Mississippi State

University, Grisham started to focus more on his studies, eventually earning a degree in accounting in 1977.

It was at Mississippi State University that Grisham's interest in law began to take shape. His courses in political science and government intrigued him, exposing him to the complexities of the legal system. The Watergate scandal was still fresh in the public consciousness, and the idea of justice, power, and accountability captivated him. It was during this period that John Grisham began to shift from dreams of the baseball diamond to dreams of the courtroom.

In 1981, after earning his law degree from the University of Mississippi School of Law, John embarked on what seemed to be a typical legal career. He began practicing law in Southaven, focusing on criminal defense and personal injury cases. However, this path was not entirely satisfying. He often found himself daydreaming about other things – characters, plots, and stories. His Southern roots and the lives of everyday people around him provided the inspiration that would eventually lead to his career as a novelist. Little did he know, the courtroom experiences he was accumulating would soon become the fuel for a literary career that would reshape his life forever.

These early years – from his boyhood in the Mississippi Delta to his journey through law school – laid the groundwork for a life that would move from small-town legal practice to international literary fame. The path was not straight, but every experience, from his father's grueling workdays to his mother's encouragement to read, would serve as a foundation for the incredible stories yet to come.

# CHAPTER TWO

## The Young Lawyer: Building a Career

In 1981, after years of study, John Grisham earned his law degree from the University of Mississippi School of Law, or "Ole Miss," as it's affectionately known. The experience of law school shaped him not just intellectually but also personally. Grisham had already developed a sharp mind, but law school refined his analytical abilities, teaching him how to dissect complex legal cases and arguments. It was also here that Grisham's interest in criminal law began to sharpen. His professors were some of the finest legal minds in the South, and their passion for justice, advocacy, and civil liberties began to influence his own career choices.

Law school wasn't easy for Grisham, and there were moments where he questioned his path. However, the training provided him with a foundation in legal reasoning and taught him how to defend clients, regardless of whether they were guilty or innocent. It was during his time at Ole Miss that he began to fully appreciate the impact that lawyers could have on people's lives. Whether in criminal cases or civil matters, the responsibility of an attorney went beyond just interpreting the law; it was about protecting rights, safeguarding freedoms, and ensuring justice was served.

When Grisham graduated, he returned to Southaven, Mississippi, and began his legal career in earnest. While law school had taught him theory, Grisham quickly realized that practicing law was something else entirely. The reality of working as a lawyer in a small Southern town was worlds apart from the courtroom dramas depicted in films and books. The cases were often mundane, *The Client*s unpredictable, and the system burdened with bureaucratic delays. Yet this was the world Grisham would immerse himself in for nearly a decade, and it would serve as fertile ground for his creative ambitions.

The early years of Grisham's legal career were spent primarily as a criminal defense attorney and handling personal injury cases. Practicing law in Mississippi in the 1980s presented its own set of challenges. The region was still recovering from the social and racial upheavals of previous decades, and systemic inequalities were ever present in the legal system. Grisham found himself navigating a world where justice was not always blind and where who you knew could often outweigh what you knew.

As a defense attorney, Grisham represented clients who came from every walk of life: poor farmers, blue-collar workers, and individuals caught up in the cycles of crime and poverty that plagued small-town America. The Mississippi courtrooms were rarely glamorous, and his cases often dealt with common crimes DUIs, petty thefts, or domestic disputes. However, the emotional toll of criminal law was something Grisham had to face head-on. He often defended people who were clearly guilty, but the job of a defense attorney is to protect the legal rights of their client, regardless of personal guilt.

These experiences were invaluable. He became intimately familiar with the inner workings of the criminal justice system, understanding both its virtues and its flaws. There were moments of success, where justice was served and a client was acquitted based on a sound legal argument. But there were just as many times when the weight of a guilty verdict or the inequities of the system were heavy. Grisham learned to navigate these complexities with skill, becoming known as a diligent and persistent lawyer.

Despite his growing reputation, Grisham often found his mind wandering away from legal briefs and depositions. Courtroom arguments, with their drama and human tension, seemed like stories waiting to be told. Each case brought him face to face with the most profound aspects of the human condition: desperation, greed, vengeance, and sometimes even hope. It wasn't long before Grisham realized that his calling might not solely lie within the courtroom but in the stories waiting to be written about it.

One case in particular, early in his career, planted the seed for what would eventually become his first novel. Grisham was sitting in court, waiting for a routine hearing, when he overheard the testimony of a 12-year-old girl who had been raped. The testimony, raw and emotionally charged, left a lasting impact on him. He began imagining how the father of such a girl might react if justice seemed out of reach. This notion of a parent taking the law into their own hands intrigued Grisham and would eventually serve as the inspiration for *A Time to kill*, his debut novel.

Though Grisham had never set out to become a writer, his experiences in the courtroom were stirring his imagination. By the mid-1980s, after a few years in practice, he decided to give writing a serious attempt. The inspiration came from a combination of his growing dissatisfaction with the legal grind and his desire to tell the stories that seemed to be everywhere around him—stories of injustice, of human complexity, and of small-town life that could be both brutal and beautiful.

Grisham's writing process was not glamorous. His legal practice kept him busy, and he had a young family to support. Writing became something he did in the early morning hours, long before the workday began. He would wake up at 5 a.m., sit down at his kitchen table with a cup of coffee, and hammer out a few pages before heading to the office. This disciplined approach allowed him to slowly, over the course of several years, complete his first novel.

The early drafts of *A Time to kill* were rough, and Grisham often doubted whether anyone would ever want to read his work. He wasn't a trained writer, and there were no immediate plans for a literary career. His initial attempts at getting published were met with rejection after rejection. Major publishing houses turned down the manuscript, uninterested in a courtroom drama set in the Deep South. But Grisham persevered, and after countless submissions, he eventually found a small publisher willing to take a chance on him.

In 1989, *A Time to kill* was published. Though the book was not an immediate bestseller, it marked the beginning of Grisham's transformation from lawyer to novelist. The novel was deeply personal, reflecting not only his experiences as a lawyer but also his understanding of the complexities of justice in a racially divided Mississippi. The story of a black man who kills the white men who raped his daughter resonated with readers in ways Grisham had not anticipated, and while the initial reception was modest, it laid the foundation for what would come next.

As Grisham balanced his law practice with his growing writing ambitions, he found himself at a crossroads. He loved the law, but the passion he once had for it was now divided with his burgeoning literary career. The worlds of fiction and reality seemed to blur, as his courtroom experiences continued to inspire his writing. But even in those early years, Grisham knew that if he wanted to succeed as a writer, he would eventually need to make a choice between the two paths.

# CHAPTER THREE

## A Time to kill: The Birth of a Writer

By the late 1980s, John Grisham was living a double life lawyer by day, aspiring writer by night. His legal career was progressing well; he had built a respectable reputation in Southaven, Mississippi, handling a range of cases from criminal defense to personal injury lawsuits. However, a deeper passion had taken root in the quiet hours of the early morning when Grisham sat down to write. Inspired by the events he had witnessed in courtrooms, he found himself returning to the same question: What if a father, seeing no hope for justice, decided to take the law into his own hands?

This question grew from a real-life experience in 1984, when Grisham had overheard the heart-wrenching testimony of a young rape victim. As he listened to the victim recount her ordeal, Grisham began to imagine a story centered around her father—a man driven to protect his daughter at all costs. This seed of an idea became the foundation of his first novel, *A Time to kill*.

Writing a novel was a massive undertaking, and Grisham was fully aware that he was venturing into uncharted territory. He had no formal training as a writer, and he wasn't connected to the world of publishing. But what he lacked in literary background, he made up for with determination and discipline. Grisham set a goal for himself: he would write one page every day, no matter how busy or tired he was from his legal work. He understood that writing a book required patience, much like building a case in court it had to be done step by step, with every word contributing to the larger narrative.

Grisham's writing process was methodical. He woke up early each morning, before heading to his law office, and dedicated two to three hours to writing. This routine became sacred, as the novel slowly took shape over the course of several years. He focused on creating characters who felt real, drawing heavily from his own experiences in the courtroom and the small-town Southern life he knew so well. *A Time to kill* reflected the complexities of the South, its racial tensions, its sense of community, and the often brutal realities of the justice system.

Set in the fictional town of Clanton, Mississippi, the novel follows the story of Carl Lee Hailey, a black man who kills two white men after they brutally rape his 10-year-old daughter. The case sparks racial unrest in the town, and Jake Brigance, an idealistic young lawyer, agrees to defend Carl Lee, despite knowing the dangers and challenges that lie ahead. Grisham poured his heart into this story, weaving together the legal drama with the intense emotions of a father seeking justice in a deeply divided society.

As Grisham worked through drafts of the manuscript, he began to feel the weight of what he was attempting to do. Writing the novel was not just an artistic endeavor; it was a personal one. He was writing about themes that mattered to him justice, race, and morality set against the backdrop of the South, a place where these issues were ever-present. But while the writing process was fulfilling, it was only the beginning of Grisham's journey. The real challenge would come when he tried to get the book published.

Once the manuscript for *A Time to kill* was completed in 1987, Grisham faced the daunting task of finding a publisher. As a first-time author with no connections in the literary world, he knew the odds were stacked against him. The publishing industry was notoriously difficult to break into, especially for unknown writers, and Grisham had no illusions about the challenges that lay ahead.

Grisham began the process by querying literary agents and publishers, sending out the manuscript to anyone who might be interested in his work. The rejections came swiftly. Most publishers weren't interested in a courtroom drama set in a small Southern town, and the racial themes of the book likely made it even harder to sell. At the time, the literary market was more focused on urban settings and popular thrillers, and Grisham's novel didn't seem to fit neatly into any established genre.

For months, Grisham faced rejection after rejection. Some publishers praised the writing but felt that the subject matter was too controversial or difficult to market. Others simply passed without explanation. The rejections were discouraging, but Grisham was not easily deterred. He believed in the story he had written, and he was determined to see it published, even if it meant exhausting every option available to him.

Finally, after numerous setbacks, Grisham caught a break. A small publisher based in New York, Wynwood Press, expressed interest in the manuscript. Wynwood was a relatively unknown company, with limited resources and little influence in the publishing world. However, they were willing to take a chance on *A Time to kill*. Grisham signed a modest contract, with no expectations of a major release or widespread success.

In 1989, *A Time to kill* was published with an initial print run of just 5,000 copies. The release was quiet there were no major promotional campaigns or book tours, and the novel didn't receive much attention from critics. Most bookstores didn't stock the book, and it was difficult for readers to even find a copy. For Grisham, the modest release was bittersweet. While he had achieved his goal of becoming a published author, the book's limited reach meant that few people would actually read it.

Grisham continued working as a lawyer, juggling his legal career with his writing ambitions. At this point, there was no indication that *A Time to kill* would ever gain traction or lead to anything beyond a small, local following. The initial sales were underwhelming, and Grisham resigned himself to the possibility that his literary career might never take off. However, the novel had planted a seed, and though it didn't bloom immediately, it would eventually lead to something much bigger.

While *A Time to kill* may not have been an instant bestseller, it did begin to attract attention in Grisham's home state of Mississippi. The book's Southern setting and themes resonated with local readers, and word of mouth began to spread, albeit slowly. Grisham made appearances at local bookstores, speaking to small groups of readers and signing copies of the novel. These early supporters, many of them friends and colleagues, were instrumental in keeping the book alive during its early days.

Grisham also found an unexpected ally in booksellers. Independent bookstores in the South began recommending the novel to customers, and some even held special events featuring Grisham. Though the sales were modest, the novel started to gain a loyal following in the region. It wasn't the explosive success Grisham had hoped for, but it was a start.

In the meantime, Grisham was already working on his second novel, a legal thriller called *The Firm*. Unlike *A Time to kill*, which was a deeply personal and regionally focused novel, *The Firm* had the potential for broader appeal. It was a fast-paced story about a young lawyer who becomes entangled in a corrupt law firm, and it had all the elements of a commercial success—suspense, intrigue, and high-stakes drama.

As Grisham continued to promote *A Time to kill* locally, he began submitting *The Firm* to publishers. This time, the response was different. The manuscript for *The Firm* attracted immediate interest, and several publishers entered a bidding war for the rights to the novel. Grisham eventually sold the rights to *The Firm* for a significant sum, and the novel was published in 1991, becoming an instant bestseller.

The success of *The Firm* had a ripple effect on *A Time to kill*. Suddenly, readers who had discovered Grisham through his second novel were eager to read his first. *A Time to kill* was reprinted and gained a new life, reaching a much wider audience than it had during its initial release.

The novel that had once been overlooked and rejected by major publishers was now being hailed as a powerful debut, and Grisham's career as a writer was officially launched.

In the span of just two years, Grisham had gone from an unknown lawyer with a passion for writing to one of the most successful authors in the country. *A Time to kill* may not have been an overnight success, but it laid the foundation for everything that followed. It was the novel that established Grisham's voice as a storyteller and set the stage for a career that would eventually make him a household name.

# CHAPTER FOUR

## The Firm and Beyond: Rise to Literary Stardom

By the early 1990s, John Grisham was still practicing law in Southaven, Mississippi, and balancing his budding writing career. His first novel, *A Time to kill*, had been released to a lukewarm reception, but it wasn't enough to propel Grisham into literary fame. That would all change with the release of his second novel, *The Firm*, in 1991.

Unlike his first book, which was deeply rooted in the racial and legal dynamics of the South, *The Firm* was a taut legal thriller that focused on Mitch McDeere, a young Harvard Law graduate who becomes entangled in the dark secrets of a corrupt Memphis law firm. The novel combined elements of suspense, high-stakes drama, and moral tension, making it more universally appealing to a broader audience. Whereas *A Time to kill* had struggled to find a market, *The Firm* hit all the right notes for a commercial success.

Grisham had learned from the struggles he faced in trying to publish his first novel, and with *The Firm*, he took a different approach. Even before the novel was published, there was a growing buzz around the manuscript, and

Hollywood studios quickly took notice. In a groundbreaking move, Paramount Pictures purchased the film rights to *The Firm* for a staggering $600,000 an unheard-of sum for a sophomore novel by a relatively unknown author. This deal set the stage for what would become one of the most successful film adaptations of a book in the 1990s, starring Tom Cruise in the lead role.

The film rights were sold before the book even hit the shelves, creating anticipation and excitement around the novel's release. When *The Firm* was finally published in 1991, it exploded onto the literary scene. The novel became an instant bestseller, spending an astounding 47 weeks on the *New York Times* bestseller list. Readers were captivated by the fast-paced plot, the moral dilemmas faced by McDeere, and the tense, page-turning action that propelled the story forward. Grisham had found the perfect formula for a legal thriller, and *The Firm* was its first successful embodiment.

The commercial success of *The Firm* was overwhelming, and it catapulted Grisham into the ranks of America's most popular authors. For the first time, Grisham began to see the possibility of a full-time career as a writer, but the success of the novel came with its own set of pressures. Grisham suddenly found himself in the public eye, with expectations from readers, publishers, and the film industry all weighing on him. But rather than shy away from the challenge, Grisham embraced it, using the momentum of *The Firm* to launch what would become one of the most prolific literary careers of the decade.

For Grisham, the success of *The Firm* was life-changing. He had gone from being a small-town lawyer with a passion for writing to one of the most sought-after authors in the country. But with that success came a major decision: Should he continue practicing law, or should he pursue writing full-time?

By the time *The Firm* was released, Grisham was already working on his third novel, *The Pelican Brief*, but he hadn't yet made the leap to full-time writing. Law was not just a profession for Grisham; it was a significant part of his identity. He had spent years building his legal career and had a deep connection to the courtroom and the people he represented. Giving up that part of his life was not an easy decision, but the demands of his writing career were becoming impossible to ignore.

As *The Firm* continued to climb the bestseller charts, Grisham realized that he could no longer balance his legal work with his writing. The success of the novel had opened doors for him that he had never imagined, and opportunities for film adaptations, book deals, and media appearances were flooding in. The legal cases that had once defined his daily life now seemed like distractions from the larger, more creative work he wanted to pursue.

In 1991, Grisham made the difficult decision to retire from law and focus on writing full-time. It was a decision that many of his colleagues and friends found surprising, especially given his success as a lawyer. But for Grisham, the choice was clear. Writing had become more than just a hobby it was his true passion, and he knew that if he wanted to continue growing as an author, he needed to devote himself fully to it.

Grisham's transition to full-time writing was seamless, thanks in large part to the financial success of *The Firm*. With the royalties from book sales and the film rights deal,

Grisham no longer had to worry about the day-to-day stresses of running a law practice. Instead, he could focus entirely on crafting stories that would capture the imaginations of readers around the world.

Despite leaving the courtroom behind, Grisham never lost his connection to the legal world. His experiences as a lawyer continued to inform his writing, providing him with a deep well of material to draw from. The themes of justice, corruption, and moral ambiguity that he had encountered during his legal career became the cornerstone of his novels, and his unique perspective as a former attorney set him apart from other thriller writers.

With the success of *The Firm*, Grisham quickly established himself as the preeminent writer of legal thrillers. But it wasn't just the popularity of his books that set him apart it was the formula he had developed for telling compelling, high-stakes stories that kept readers coming back for more.

Grisham's novels typically featured ordinary people lawyers, judges, jurors who found themselves caught up in extraordinary circumstances. His protagonists were often young and idealistic, entering the legal profession with a strong sense of right and wrong, only to be confronted with the harsh realities of corruption, greed, and moral compromise. These characters were relatable to readers because they were flawed and human, struggling to navigate a world where justice was not always served.

At the heart of Grisham's novels was the tension between law and morality. His characters often faced difficult choices, where the right thing to do legally was not always the right thing to do morally. This moral complexity resonated with readers, who appreciated the ethical dilemmas Grisham's characters faced. Unlike traditional crime thrillers, where good and evil were clearly defined, Grisham's novels operated in the gray areas of the legal system, where justice was not always black and white.

Grisham's success also stemmed from his ability to write tightly plotted, fast-paced stories that kept readers on the edge of their seats. His novels were page-turners, filled with suspense and unexpected twists, but they were also deeply grounded in the legal world. Grisham's background as a lawyer gave his books a level of authenticity that readers trusted. He knew how the legal system worked the procedures, the jargon, the power dynamics—and he used that knowledge to create realistic, immersive stories.

As Grisham's career progressed, his name became synonymous with legal thrillers. He had established a brand that readers could rely on: If they picked up a John Grisham novel, they knew they were in for a gripping, morally complex story set in the high-stakes world of the law. Grisham's books became a staple in airport bookstores, on summer reading lists, and in book clubs across the country.

But while Grisham's novels were incredibly popular, they were also critically respected. Reviewers praised his ability to tackle important social issues within the framework of a thriller, and his books were often lauded for their commentary on the American legal system. Grisham had achieved a rare balance between commercial success and literary credibility, and by the end of the 1990s, he was one of the most successful and influential authors in the world.

# CHAPTER FIVE

## Broadening Horizons: Exploring New Territories

By the dawn of the 21st century, John Grisham had firmly established himself as the king of the legal thriller. His novels had become synonymous with fast-paced plots, morally complex characters, and gripping legal drama, with millions of readers around the world eagerly anticipating each new release. Yet, after dominating the genre for more than a decade, Grisham found himself at a crossroads. The legal thriller, while immensely successful, had its limits, and Grisham was not a man content to rest on his laurels. As the new millennium dawned, he began to explore new creative territories, broadening his literary horizons and challenging both himself and his readers.

After releasing a string of successful legal thrillers throughout the 1990s, Grisham faced a growing desire to step outside the genre that had made him famous. By 2000, he had written more than a dozen novels that explored the inner workings of the legal system, but as much as he loved the law, Grisham was eager to stretch his creative muscles and explore different types of storytelling. It wasn't that he had lost interest in legal drama, but rather that he wanted to show the world and perhaps even himself that he was capable of more.

One of the first signs of this shift came with the release of *The Brethren* in 2000. Though it still centered around a legal plot, the novel diverged from Grisham's earlier works by incorporating elements of political intrigue and blackmail, marking a subtle but important departure from the purely courtroom-based drama of his earlier novels. The book was another bestseller, further solidifying Grisham's place at the top of the literary world, but it also signaled that he was not content to be pigeonholed as just a legal thriller author.

Grisham's true departure from the genre, however, came with the release of *A Painted House* in 2001. This novel, set in rural Arkansas during the 1950s, was a complete departure from the legal thrillers that had made Grisham famous. Instead of focusing on lawyers and courtrooms, *A Painted House* told the story of a young boy growing up on a cotton farm, and it was deeply influenced by Grisham's own childhood experiences in the rural South. The novel was a quiet, introspective piece of historical fiction that explored themes of family, hardship, and the loss of innocence – a far cry from the high-stakes world of legal drama that Grisham had previously mined.

Venturing Beyond Legal Thrillers, this marked a bold step for Grisham, both personally and professionally. He had proven that he could write blockbuster legal thrillers, but with *A Painted House*, he demonstrated that he was capable of much more. The novel received critical acclaim for its evocative prose and richly detailed depiction of life in the rural South, with many reviewers praising Grisham's ability to capture the rhythms and nuances of small-town life. It was a book that clearly came from the heart, and it showcased a different side of Grisham's talent – one that his readers had never seen before.

The success of *A Painted House* opened up new creative possibilities for Grisham. No longer confined to the legal thriller genre, he began to experiment with different types of stories, pushing the boundaries of his own writing. In 2001, he released *Skipping Christmas*, a lighthearted holiday novel about a family that decides to forgo the traditional Christmas festivities and instead plan a tropical getaway, only to face a series of comic misadventures. The book was a departure not only in terms of subject matter but also in tone it was fun, breezy, and humorous, showcasing Grisham's ability to write in a completely different register.

Though *Skipping Christmas* was not a serious or weighty novel, it was immensely popular, particularly around the holiday season. It was later adapted into a film, Christmas with the Kranks, starring Tim Allen and Jamie Lee Curtis, which further expanded Grisham's presence in Hollywood. While some critics dismissed *Skipping Christmas* as a lightweight, commercial endeavor, others appreciated Grisham's willingness to step outside his comfort zone and try something new. In many ways, *Skipping Christmas* was a testament to Grisham's versatility as a writer – he was able to shift from writing high-stakes legal thrillers to crafting a warm, comedic holiday story with ease.

The success of *A Painted House* and *Skipping Christmas* gave Grisham the confidence to continue exploring new genres. Over the next several years, he dabbled in a variety of different types of stories, from sports to young adult fiction, proving that his storytelling abilities were not limited to the courtroom.

In 2003, Grisham released *Bleachers*, a nostalgic novel about a high school football coach and the former players who reunite to pay their respects after his death. The book was a poignant meditation on small-town life, the passage of time, and the relationships between coaches and their players. While it didn't have the page-turning suspense of Grisham's legal thrillers, *Bleachers* resonated with readers, particularly those who had grown up in small towns and understood the deep connection between football and community.

Grisham's interest in sports also led him to write *Playing for Pizza* in 2007, a lighthearted novel about a washed-up NFL quarterback who finds redemption playing for a football team in Italy. The book was a blend of sports drama and travelogue, and while it didn't achieve the same level of success as his legal thrillers, it was an enjoyable departure from his usual fare. Grisham's passion for football, which had been a part of his life since childhood, was evident in both *Bleachers* and *Playing for Pizza*, and these books allowed him to indulge his love of the game while still telling compelling stories.

In addition to his ventures into sports fiction, Grisham also made a foray into young adult literature with the release of his *Theodore Boone* series. The first book in the series, *Theodore Boone: Kid Lawyer*, was published in 2010 and introduced readers to a precocious 13-year-old boy who dreams of becoming a lawyer. The series was aimed at younger readers, but it retained the legal intrigue and suspense that had made Grisham famous, albeit with a lighter tone and more accessible language. The *Theodore Boone* books were a hit with young readers and parents alike, and they introduced a new generation to Grisham's storytelling.

Throughout the 2000s, Grisham continued to write legal thrillers as well, ensuring that his loyal fan base was not disappointed. Novels like *The Summons* (2002), *The King of Torts* (2003), and *The Appeal* (2008) were all bestsellers, and they demonstrated that Grisham had not lost his touch when it came to crafting page-turning legal dramas. But even as he continued to dominate the legal thriller genre, it was clear that Grisham was no longer content to be defined by it. He was a writer who was constantly evolving, constantly looking for new challenges, and constantly pushing himself to explore new creative avenues.

While Grisham's literary career was flourishing during the 2000s, his involvement in Hollywood also reached new heights. Many of his earlier novels, such as *The Firm*, *The Pelican Brief*, and *A Time to kill*, had been successfully adapted into films in the 1990s, but Grisham's relationship with the film industry continued to evolve throughout the next decade.

One of the most significant film adaptations during this period was *The Runaway Jury*, which was released in 2003. The film, based on Grisham's 1996 novel of the same name, starred John Cusack, Gene Hackman, and Dustin Hoffman, and was a legal thriller that explored the concept of jury tampering in a high-stakes tobacco lawsuit. While the film received mixed reviews, it was another example of Grisham's work translating to the big screen, and it reinforced his status as one of the most adaptable authors in Hollywood.

Grisham's involvement in film adaptations extended beyond simply selling the rights to his books. As his influence in the industry grew, he began to take a more active role in the adaptation process, working closely with filmmakers to ensure that his stories were faithfully translated to the screen. He had learned from the experiences of the early adaptations of his work and became more selective about the projects he chose to pursue.

In 2004, Grisham's *Skipping Christmas* was adapted into the film *Christmas with the Kranks*, a family-friendly holiday comedy that, while not a critical success, performed well at the box office. Grisham's ability to write stories that could easily transition from page to screen was a testament to his understanding of narrative structure and character development. He had an innate sense of what made a story compelling, and that skill translated well to the visual medium of film.

By the end of the 2000s, Grisham had become one of the most successful authors in the world, not only in terms of book sales but also in terms of his influence on popular culture. His novels had been translated into more than 40 languages, and his books had sold more than 300 million copies worldwide. His success in Hollywood only added to his cultural cachet, and he had become one of the few authors whose name alone could sell both books and movie tickets.

# CHAPTER SIX

## The Established Author: Legacy and Continued Success

In the 2010s, John Grisham, by now a household name and one of the most successful authors of his generation, returned to the genre that had made him famous: the legal thriller. After experimenting with various genres and writing styles throughout the 2000s, Grisham found that his audience still had a massive appetite for the kind of high-stakes courtroom dramas that had first catapulted him into the literary spotlight.

While his experimentation in other genres had earned him critical acclaim and broadened his readership, it was clear that legal thrillers remained his forte. With renewed vigor, Grisham returned to the familiar territory of the legal world, crafting stories that tackled contemporary issues within the framework of the legal system.

In 2011, Grisham released *The Litigators*, a novel that combined his signature courtroom drama with a biting satirical take on the personal injury law industry. The novel's protagonists, a group of unscrupulous ambulance chasers, provided a humorous contrast to the more morally upright lawyers that had often populated Grisham's earlier works. *The Litigators* was a commercial success, proving that Grisham's formula for legal thrillers still resonated with readers even after two decades of dominance.

As the decade progressed, Grisham continued to churn out legal thrillers that captivated his audience. Novels like *Gray Mountain* (2014) and *The Whistler* (2016) demonstrated Grisham's ability to evolve within the genre. *Gray Mountain* explored the complexities of environmental law, focusing on the coal mining industry in Appalachia, while *The Whistler* delved into judicial corruption and the dark side of Native American casino operations. These novels showcased Grisham's ability to weave social and political commentary into his legal thrillers, keeping the genre fresh and relevant.

One of the hallmarks of Grisham's later career has been his increasing focus on social issues, using his novels as a platform to shed light on important topics such as corruption, environmental degradation, wrongful convictions, and the flaws within the justice system. While many of his early works had already hinted at his interest in social justice most notably *A Time to kill* this focus became more pronounced in his post-2010 works.

In Sycamore Row (2013), a sequel to *A Time to kill*, Grisham returned to the racially charged atmosphere of the Deep South, exploring themes of inheritance, race, and justice. The novel followed the fallout from a wealthy white man's decision to leave his fortune to his Black housekeeper, triggering a fierce legal battle. *Sycamore Row* not only satisfied fans of *A Time to kill* but also introduced a new generation of readers to the complex racial dynamics that still plagued the South.

Grisham also used his fiction to explore the issue of wrongful convictions, a topic that had long fascinated him. In *The Innocent Man: Murder and Injustice in a Small Town* (2006), a non-fiction work, he had already delved into the subject, but it was through his legal thrillers that he continued to shine a light on the failures of the justice system. Novels like *The Confession* (2010) and *The Guardians* (2019) tackled the issue head-on, with both books centering on the plight of innocent men wrongfully convicted of crimes they did not commit.

In *The Guardians*, Grisham introduced readers to a fictionalized version of the Innocence Project, a non-profit organization dedicated to exonerating the wrongfully convicted. The novel followed Cullen Post, a lawyer and Episcopal priest, as he fought to free a man who had spent more than two decades on death row for a murder he did not commit. The novel was both a gripping legal thriller and a searing indictment of the flaws in the American criminal justice system.

Grisham's willingness to tackle such weighty subjects has earned him praise not only as a master storyteller but also as a writer unafraid to confront the darker aspects of society. His novels have become more than just entertaining page-turners; they are vehicles for exploring and challenging the status quo, prompting readers to think critically about the world around them.

As Grisham's career flourished, so too did his philanthropic endeavors. Throughout his life, Grisham has been a passionate advocate for various causes, particularly those related to justice, education, and literacy. He has used his considerable wealth and influence to support numerous charitable organizations, both in the United States and abroad.

One of Grisham's most significant contributions has been his involvement with the Innocence Project, an organization that works to exonerate individuals who have been wrongfully convicted of crimes. Inspired by the real-life cases of wrongful conviction that he had encountered during his legal career and research for his novels, Grisham became a vocal supporter of the organization's mission. In addition to donating money, Grisham has used his platform to raise awareness about the issue of wrongful convictions, often incorporating themes of justice and redemption into his fiction.

Grisham's philanthropy also extends to education. As a former lawyer who benefited from a strong educational foundation, Grisham has long been a proponent of improving access to quality education for all. He and his wife, Renee, have funded numerous scholarships for students in need, particularly in his home state of

Mississippi. They have also supported efforts to improve public schools in underserved communities, recognizing that education is one of the most effective ways to break the cycle of poverty.

In the literary world, Grisham's influence is undeniable. As one of the best-selling authors of all time, he has inspired countless aspiring writers to pursue careers in fiction. His success has shown that it is possible to achieve both critical and commercial acclaim, and his work has been a touchstone for writers interested in exploring legal and social issues through fiction.

Grisham has also been a champion of literacy, supporting initiatives to promote reading and writing among young people. He has donated millions of books to schools and libraries, particularly in rural areas where access to literature is often limited. Through his philanthropy, Grisham has sought to share his love of storytelling with future generations, ensuring that the power of the written word continues to thrive.

As John Grisham reflects on his career, he has much to be proud of. Over the course of three decades, he has written dozens of novels, sold more than 300 million copies of his books, and seen his work adapted into major motion pictures. His novels have been translated into multiple languages, making him a global literary phenomenon. Yet, despite his immense success, Grisham remains humble and grounded, always quick to credit his readers for their continued support.

In interviews, Grisham has often spoken about the unexpected nature of his success. When he first wrote *A Time to kill*, he had no idea that it would lead to a career as one of the world's most successful authors. At the time, he was simply a young lawyer with a passion for storytelling, trying to juggle his legal practice with his writing. Even after the success of *The Firm*, Grisham was cautious about leaving the law behind completely, unsure if his success as a writer would last. Now, decades later, Grisham can look back on his career with a sense of accomplishment and gratitude.

As for the future, Grisham shows no signs of slowing down. In recent interviews, he has expressed his desire to continue writing for as long as possible, stating that he still has many stories left to tell. While legal thrillers will always be his bread and butter, Grisham remains open to exploring new genres and topics, much as he did in the 2000s. His curiosity and passion for storytelling continue to drive him, and he is constantly looking for new ways to challenge himself as a writer.

Grisham has also hinted at the possibility of returning to non-fiction. His experience writing *The Innocent Man* was deeply rewarding, and he has expressed interest in exploring other true crime stories in the future. Given his background in law and his keen understanding of the justice system, it seems likely that any future non-fiction work from Grisham would focus on issues of justice and social inequality.

As Grisham looks to the future, his legacy as one of the most successful and influential authors of his generation is already secure. His impact on the literary world is undeniable, and his contributions to the causes of justice, education, and literacy will continue to resonate for years to come. For John Grisham, the past three decades have been a remarkable journey and yet, in many ways, it feels as though he is just getting started.

# CHAPTER SEVEN

## The Grisham Effect

Few authors have left as indelible a mark on a genre as John Grisham has on the legal thriller. Since the release of his breakthrough novel, *The Firm*, in 1991, Grisham has not only redefined the modern legal thriller but also elevated it into a mainstream literary genre that has captivated millions of readers worldwide. His intricate plotting, engaging characters, and ability to turn the dry procedures of law into riveting storytelling have changed the way the public perceives both literature and the legal profession.

Before Grisham, legal fiction existed, but it had not been perfected in a way that blended mass-market appeal with authentic legal insight. Authors such as Scott Turow and Erle Stanley Gardner the creator of *Perry Mason* certainly laid the groundwork, but it was Grisham who brought the genre into the mainstream and turned it into a global phenomenon. With the publication of *The Firm*, readers were introduced to a gripping world where the intricacies of law, corporate greed, and personal ethics intersected with pulse-pounding suspense.

Grisham's debut novel, *A Time to kill*, was an earnest and heartfelt exploration of Southern racial tensions and courtroom drama. However, it wasn't until *The Firm* that he truly found his commercial voice, fusing a thriller's fast paced tension with a backdrop of legal intrigue. This combination of a high-stakes courtroom narrative and personal jeopardy would come to define the "Grisham formula" and set the standard for legal thrillers for decades to come.

Grisham's success sparked a surge of interest in legal thrillers, leading to the rise of a sub-genre populated by writers attempting to emulate his style. The genre began to focus not only on lawyers in courtrooms but also on the legal entanglements that occur behind the scenes—in law firms, boardrooms, and everyday life. From novels about class-action lawsuits to the seedy underbelly of corporate law, Grisham's influence helped expand the genre's thematic scope, and many aspiring authors found inspiration in his work.

Beyond the formulaic components that Grisham popularized, one of his greatest impacts on the genre has been his ability to humanize the law. In his books, legal cases are never just abstract battles fought between faceless entities. Instead, they are deeply personal struggles in which the fate of individuals hangs in the balance. Whether it's a small-town lawyer fighting for justice or a whistleblower exposing corporate corruption, Grisham's characters face moral dilemmas that resonate with readers on a profound level.

Additionally, Grisham's influence has been felt in the way that the legal profession is portrayed in fiction. Lawyers are often shown as more than just legal minds they are fully fleshed-out characters with personal flaws, ethical dilemmas, and a strong sense of justice. This humanizing of the legal profession has contributed to a broader cultural understanding of what it means to be a lawyer and how the law intersects with morality, ethics, and society.

In short, Grisham transformed the legal thriller from a niche sub-genre into one of the most popular and enduring forms of contemporary fiction. His success paved the way for countless other writers to explore the world of law, and the legal thriller genre has flourished as a result.

John Grisham's influence extends far beyond the literary world. His novels, many of which have been adapted into successful films and television shows, have left an indelible mark on popular culture. Through these adaptations, Grisham's narratives have reached audiences who may not typically read legal thrillers, solidifying his position as a cultural icon.

One of the most significant ways Grisham has influenced popular culture is through his depictions of lawyers and the legal system. From *The Firm* to *The Rainmaker*, his stories have shaped the way lawyers are viewed by the public. In many ways, Grisham's portrayal of the legal profession reflects the tension between idealism and pragmatism that many lawyers experience in real life. His characters are often torn between doing what is legally permissible and doing what is morally right, a conflict that resonates with readers and viewers alike.

Films like *The Pelican Brief* (1993), *A Time to kill* (1996), and *The Rainmaker* (1997) have helped to cement the public's fascination with legal dramas. These adaptations, often featuring A-list actors like Tom Cruise, Julia Roberts, Matthew McConaughey, and Matt Damon, brought Grisham's stories to life and amplified his impact on popular culture. The courtroom scenes in these films tense, dramatic, and full of moral ambiguity have become some of the most iconic depictions of legal battles in modern cinema. Moreover, these films have contributed to a cultural fascination with the courtroom as a stage for dramatic conflict, where justice is served (or denied) in front of an audience of jurors, judges, and spectators.

Grisham's influence on popular culture has also extended to the legal profession itself. Many young lawyers and law students have cited his novels as an inspiration for pursuing a career in law. While real-life legal practice is often far more mundane than the high-stakes world depicted in

Grisham's books, his stories nonetheless capture the excitement and intellectual challenge that draw many people to the profession. His novels also highlight the moral and ethical dimensions of practicing law, reminding readers that the pursuit of justice is often fraught with difficult choices.

In addition to inspiring individuals to enter the legal profession, Grisham's work has sparked public debates about important legal and social issues. Through his fiction, Grisham has explored topics such as corporate corruption, environmental degradation, wrongful convictions, and the death penalty. These issues, which are often based on real-world cases, have prompted readers to think critically about the flaws in the legal system and the broader societal impact of legal decisions.

For example, *The Confession* (2010) and *The Innocent Man* (2006) brought widespread attention to the issue of wrongful convictions and the death penalty. In both works, Grisham uses the legal thriller format to highlight the devastating consequences of a flawed justice system. *The Innocent Man* was particularly impactful, as it was

Grisham's first non-fiction work and detailed the true story of Ron Williamson, an Oklahoma man wrongfully convicted of murder. The book helped to raise awareness about the dangers of relying on circumstantial evidence and the importance of organizations like the Innocence Project, which works to exonerate the wrongfully convicted.

Grisham's ability to tackle weighty social issues within the framework of a legal thriller has not only kept his readers engaged but has also contributed to broader discussions about justice, fairness, and the role of the legal system in society.

As John Grisham continues to write and publish novels, his legacy as one of the most influential authors of the modern era is already well established. His contributions to the legal thriller genre, popular culture, and social discourse have left an indelible mark on the literary landscape.

One of Grisham's most significant achievements is his ability to make complex legal concepts accessible to a wide audience. While his novels often delve into the intricacies of the law, they are written in a way that is engaging and easy to understand, even for readers who have no background in the legal profession. This ability to bridge the gap between the legal world and the general public has made his work not only entertaining but also educational. Readers come away from his books with a greater understanding of how the legal system works and the ethical dilemmas that lawyers face.

Grisham's novels have also demonstrated the power of storytelling to effect change. By using his platform to address important social issues, he has helped to raise awareness about the flaws in the justice system and the need for reform. His work with organizations like the Innocence Project, along with his advocacy for criminal justice reform, has extended his influence beyond the pages of his books and into the real world.

In addition to his literary accomplishments, Grisham's success as a best-selling author has inspired countless writers to follow in his footsteps. His ability to craft compelling narratives and build suspense has set a high standard for aspiring authors in the legal thriller genre. Many of today's most popular legal thriller writers, such as

Scott Turow, Lisa Scottoline, and Michael Connelly, have acknowledged Grisham's influence on their work.

Grisham's legacy is also evident in the numerous film and television adaptations of his books. While not all of these adaptations have been critical successes, they have nonetheless contributed to the enduring popularity of his stories and have introduced his work to new audiences. In particular, films like *The Firm* and *A Time to kill* have become classics of the legal thriller genre and continue to be referenced in popular culture.

As Grisham's career continues, there is no doubt that his legacy will only grow. His ability to captivate readers with gripping legal dramas, while also addressing important social issues, has made him one of the most influential authors of his generation. Whether he is writing about corporate greed, environmental degradation, or the fight for justice, Grisham's work resonates with readers because it speaks to the universal struggle for fairness and the pursuit of truth.

Printed in Great Britain
by Amazon